Never Alone

JOAN WINMILL BROWN

The C.R. Gibson Company,
Norwalk, Connecticut 06856

Hope for All
Tomorrows

IN a world that can often seem uncaring—unaware of our innermost fears—these words of John Greenleaf Whittier speak of our Creator's concern for each one of us:

"Behind the cloud the starlight lurks,
Through showers the sunbeams fall;
For God who loveth all His works,
Has left His Hope with all."

Hope is one of the most glorious words in the English language, for it speaks of trust and reliance in the future. Today may seem dark, impenetrable, the future bleak—but out there is that glimmer of hope; like the warm, gleaming light of a candle, illuminating our way.

This gift from God is not elusive, if we are trusting Him for our todays, and the future. The Bible's more than seventy references to hope assure us that if we accept the greatest gift that God wishes to give us through His Son—eternal life—then all our days can be colored with the radiant knowledge that we are not alone: Our Lord is with us each moment.

The Psalmist in the Forty–second Psalm, asks this question:

"Why art thou cast down, O my soul? and why are thou disquieted in me? hope thou in God: for I shall yet praise him for the help of his countenance."

How easily most of us can identify with the Psalmist. He had his highs and lows, yet he knew the Lord would not forsake him. In spite of any problems, he had many reasons for praising God for His help.

I was reminded of our Lord's care for us when I listened recently to my sister. She told me that God had been with her at a time of great need.

"It was amazing, Joan. I just did not feel lonely. I had always dreaded the day I would have to be in this house on my own, but when Mother was taken to the hospital it was as if God were by my side. I just did not feel lonely."

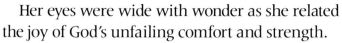

Her eyes were wide with wonder as she related the joy of God's unfailing comfort and strength.

"I am still amazed and thankful to Him for His loving care of both of us."

My sister's worst fears had been calmed by God's presence. She had found that His grace *was* sufficient.

We all face times of great loneliness. It invades our lives, creating a void we feel can never be filled. It sweeps over us not only in the privacy of our homes, but also on crowded streets. We look at other people and wonder if they, too, ever feel lonely.

Some people can hide their true feelings more successfully than others, but if each person were honest, they would admit to times of loneliness and fear of the future. If we could see beyond the exterior, into their hearts, we would find there the same longings and insecurities that are so real to each one of us.

However, none of us has to walk alone. That aching void can be filled with the presence of God.

"I will not leave you comfortless: I will come to you." (Jn. 14:18)

Whatever age you are, the problem of loneliness can surface. The teenager at high school or college may find it hard to relate to others; the young mother, restricted to her home because of small children, may struggle through times of despondency; the businessman, steeped in problems of escalating competition, and perhaps having to travel and face many lonely nights in hotel rooms, may feel overwhelmed; the older person, living alone, and feeling no one really cares, may feel abandoned. These are just a few examples of the voids that so many of us need to fill.

Loneliness *is* a major problem, but to know that God is with us *constantly* can alleviate that pain.

In Scotland, the name of Alexander MacLaren is well known. MacLaren was a dynamic preacher who loved to tell the story of an incident that occurred when he was a young boy and had left home to take a job in Glasgow. Since his weekends were free, he did not feel completely cut off from his family. He could return home at the end of the week.

But it was a long walk home. There were no street lights, and according to legend, the valley through which he had to walk was filled with evil spirits. During his first week away from home, the thought of the valley was always with him. As he worked, his mind conjured up all kinds of terrors, and he became more and more frightened.

Finally, the weekend arrived, and he had to muster all the courage he could find to start out on his journey home. Each step in the darkness brought him closer and closer to that dreaded valley. When he began the descent into it, his heart was beating so wildly he feared he would not have the strength to go on.

Then, in the darkness, he heard a familiar voice calling to him. Listening for a few seconds, he realized it was his father.

"Alex—I've come to walk through the valley with you!"

Imagine his relief, knowing he was not alone— that his father would be by his side to help him face the darkness.

So, too, God is by our side in whatever darkness we may find ourselves. He wants us to trust Him to light our way.

"For thou wilt light my candle: the Lord my God will enlighten my darkness." (Ps. 18:28)

Therefore, when fear comes raging into our lives, we must face it head on—then hand it over completely to God and accept His help. Sometimes it may seem slow in coming—but it will come eventually.

The disciples felt as if the Lord had abandoned them in the midst of the great storm on the Sea of Galilee. Their small, fragile boat seemed totally inadequate against such a force, and Jesus was nowhere to be seen. Then, in the distance, through the driving wind and rain, they saw Him walking toward them—on the water! "Impossible," they thought—yet it was true.

"Impossible," we say, too. "God can never solve my problems or take away my fear." But it isn't impossible. In the most impossible times of our lives, God comes and quiets the storm of turmoil within us, saying, *Be of good cheer: it is I; be not afraid."* (Mk. 6:50)

You Are Loved

THE reading had gone well—or so I thought. Standing in the middle of the stage of a deserted theater, I looked hopefully over the footlights to the director.

"Nice reading, Joan...but you aren't exactly right for the part. Next..."

I walked off the stage, feeling the stinging humiliation of rejection. For a then young, aspiring actress I was devastated. I had been so sure I was perfect for the part. On my way home, I thought of all that could have been wrong with me. Perhaps I had chosen the wrong hairstyle. I looked in a mirror and knew it must have been my nose. Inferiority reared its ugly head and made me feel a lesser creature.

Years later, after having played many roles, I was involved in a production of a movie and sat in on the casting. We had gone over and over the script, defining just what types we were looking for. Therefore, when the audition started, we had a very clear picture of what each character should look like, and what qualities were necessary. Each time one of the hopeful actors or actresses read, I wanted desperately for that person to have the part—remembering my days of giving everything I had to offer, and then being turned down. For an actor or actress all you have is "you," and if "you" is not right, there is nothing to fall back on. The salesman can at least blame the product he has attempted to sell.

I wish I had been able to sit in on an audition from the producer's side years before, for then I would have understood and accepted my rejections more easily.

In our lives, whether it is because we are not quite "right for the part," or whether it is because someone does not respond to us as we feel they should, we need to have an assurance of our worth. The knowledge that we are God's creation—not a haphazardly put together creature—should be uppermost in our minds.

The most difficult emotion for many of us to face and conquer *is* the feeling of rejection. Everyone, at some time or another, has encountered rejection, whether it be from one you love, in the work place, or because of physical appearance.

Yet, each one of us has been wonderfully made by our Creator. When you are despondent, look at your hands. There you see ten fingerprints that no one else on earth owns. In the files of the FBI in Washington, no other fingerprints match yours. A God who cares enough for such details must love you.

God has given different gifts to each of us. Instead of feeling rejected or inferior, we should make the most of these talents. Always remember that *you* are unique. Special. There will never be another you. You are loved by Him!

When we talk of human love, we often find that it is conditional. But God's love is absolute and unconditional. When we fail, or others reject us, He remains the same, understanding the hurts and wanting to reassure us that He cares.

The parable of the lost sheep is one that always speaks to me of the importance of each person. In Luke, Chapter Fifteen, we read of the shepherd being so concerned for the one lost sheep that he leaves the other ninety-nine to find it. When the sheep is found, there is great rejoicing. Through this parable God shows us that we are surrounded by His questing love for us. We are like that lost sheep until we come into the full realization of

God's unconditional love for us. But He never intrudes into our lives. He waits patiently for us to reach out and accept this love of His.

When we receive this gift, we have a solid foundation from which we can operate in today's often critical, unfeeling world. Sensitivity is sometimes thought of as a weakness. If we take our sensitivity to the Lord and ask Him to use it to help others—it can be turned into a strength.

Shakespeare said, "They jest at scars, who never felt a wound." Take all the wounds of your life and give them to God. It is amazing what He will do with them—and with you!

A broken relationship with someone you love is a hurt that goes so deeply that we find it hard to express in mere words. Marriages break up—perhaps a divorce ensues—and the experience of a broken home is utterly devastating. The traumas that people, so often alone, have to face today can shatter lives, and often we come to the place where we feel there is no hope.

Having once reached such a point of desperation in my own life, when it seemed utterly worthless, makes me understand how a person can feel this way. But I reached out to the Shepherd whose Love infiltrated my despondency and brought new hope. When I read the Twenty–third Psalm—one I have known for so long, but never applied to my own life—I could then joyously say, *"The Lord is* my *Shepherd; I shall not want..."*

He is the only One who can abide deep within our hearts and show us that beyond the hurts there can be a fulfilling affinity with Him. Prayer—not the formal prayers that only skim the surface, but the honest, childlike prayer of one talking to a beloved Heavenly Father— breaks through the dejection. When we realize that God is always waiting to affirm and love us, we are able to find the resiliency and the strength to pick ourselves up and go on—knowing we are not alone.

"The Lord is nigh unto all them that call upon him..." (Ps. 145:18)

He understands the agony of rejection, because He, too, was rejected. How many have rejected His love? Because His Son suffered for us, we can know we are truly loved.

"...the God of love and peace shall be with you." (2 Cor. 13:11)

The Triumph of
God's Love

IN a gloomy prison in France in the eighteenth century, a young woman sang of her love for God. Many would consider her life a failure because she was to spend the rest of her life incarcerated because of her beliefs.

The imprisoned Madam Guyon did not consider herself a failure because she believed that she was living according to the will of God.

She had lost a three-year-old daughter. Madam Guyon herself had been badly disfigured by smallpox. And, because of absolute, undeniable faith in a personal, living God, she was banished for the rest of her life to the dreaded Bastille prison in Paris. Within her dungeon, Madam Guyon wrote many books of inspiration and poetry that touch lives to this day. God was with her in her times of great sufferings, and she knew His presence would never fail her.

> *"To me remains nor place nor time;*
> *My country is in every clime.*
> *I can be calm and free from care*
> *On any shore since God is there."*

When we are suddenly faced with disappointment or failure, the loneliness can almost destroy our lives. In a world that worships success, it seems as if we will be judged by our peers forever. Sometimes they tell us that we must have done something wrong, for God to have allowed these events to have happened. This is one of the unkindest judgments. To me, it seems that sometimes He allows unfortunate circumstances to occur so that others—seeing the way we survive through our faith—can learn from them, too.

Because our work or plans have failed does not mean that God has abandoned us. It may feel like it. There may seem to be no answer to our prayers. A sense of being in an unending wilderness may envelop us. But through it all, we may be confident He is working out what is best for us. We can cry out to Him our 'whys?'. He hears and understands honest, direct prayers that come deep from within our hearts.

"The Lord hath heard my supplication: the Lord will receive my prayer." (Ps. 6:9)

The greatest failure that became a triumph was the Cross. Imagine how the disciples must have felt that first Good Friday. They had seen their Lord die, and all that they had come to believe in had died with Him. The loneliness of their experience was the ultimate. Gloom and despair entered their hearts until that glorious third day when Mary Magdalene saw her risen Lord.

Often when we feel that God is the farthest from us He is closest. On the road to Emmaus, after the Crucifixion, two of the disciples were walking along—feeling desolate. Their world had come to an end. When Someone began to walk with them, they did not realize it was the risen Jesus.

So too, in our grief we often do not realize that He is close to us, wanting to commune. We are too blinded by our tears to realize He is there.

As someone once said, out of all the heartaches we go through we either become "bitter or better." Bitterness can overwhelm and destroy the gifts that God has given to us. Bitterness toward a person, or persons, who may have been instrumental in causing our failure, can only hurt *us*.

❧

If anyone should have felt bitter toward his enemies, it could easily have been the defeated General Robert E. Lee. Retreating into Virginia after he had lost 30,000 of his men at the Battle of Gettysburg, Lee was riding past a wounded Union soldier when he heard him shout, "Hurray for the Union!" The General dismounted and went over to the soldier with a look of great compassion. The soldier wrote later:

"He extended his hand toward me and said a few kind words of comfort. If I live a thousand years, I shall never forget the expression on General Lee's face. There he was, defeated, retiring from a field that had cost him and his cause almost their last hope, and yet he stopped to give solace to a wounded soldier of the opposition who had taunted him as he passed by."

When General Lee left, the soldier, filled with awe by the compassion he had received, cried himself to sleep.

"Love your enemies, bless them that curse you..." (Mt. 5:44)

God's compassion for us encircles the life of each one of us. The meaning of the word compassion becomes even more beautiful, when we relate it to God's love for us. It is derived from the Latin 'com'—together, plus 'pati'—to suffer. God suffers with us.

"His compassions fail not. They are new every morning: great is thy faithfulness." (Lam. 3:22,23)

God's "Rest"
In the Music
of Our Lives

O UR lives are designed by God. We can compare them to the composing of a great concerto. Each note is vital to the creation of the whole work.

In the making of music, the conductor knows the importance of a "rest." For a brief time the music ceases, but the conductor continues to beat the time. Then, the music begins again. Each musician knows the importance too, of the "rest." John Ruskin, the Victorian writer, captured the meaning of these "interruptions" we sometimes have to face:

"Not without design does God write the music of our lives. But be it ours to learn the time and not be dismayed at the 'rests.' They are not to be slurred, not to be omitted, not to destroy the melody, nor to change the keynote. If we look up, God Himself will beat the time for us. With the eye on Him, we shall strike the next note full and clear."

Each one of us knows the importance of taking a vacation. Planning where we will go, the places we will visit, where we shall stay all add to the pleasure of a needed rest from our everyday activities. But sometimes we find that we are taken away from the mainstream of life—not of our own choosing, but because of illness—and *made* to take a "rest." We feel helpless: dependent on others—doctors, nurses—to bring about our healing. And if we are not looking to God for our strength and courage, we tend to fear the loneliness.

Only God can understand our fears. He is waiting to minister to us in our sickness. His comfort and tenderness is far greater than even the most loving and understanding of those closest to us.

At times when I have experienced illness, I definitely would not have chosen it. It has interrupted my plans and I have experienced fear in having to take an enforced "rest" in my life. I have gone through all the emotions of anger, sorrow and questioning, but when acceptance finally has come, it has been brought about only through close fellowship with my Lord. He has heard my cries, my fears, and He has filled me with His love. During those times, I have been drawn closer to Him and have learned more of His mercy and compassion than at any time when I was in good health. The loneliness of illness has been turned in a glorious, deeper relationship with the Lord.

In Mark, Chapter Five, I am always inspired by the account of the woman who had been ill for twelve years and believed that if only she could reach out and touch Jesus as He passed by, she would be made whole. The words indicating she told Him all the truth about herself have been an example for me. It is only when I have been completely truthful with Him that I have experienced His peace and acceptance of whatever circumstance has come into my life. Knowing my innermost thoughts and fears, He comes in to calm my troubled mind.

"Fear thou not; for I am with thee: be not dismayed; for I am thy God: I will strengthen thee; yea, I

will help thee; yea, I will uphold thee with the right hand of my righteousness." (Isa. 41:10)

God's promises to us that He *is* with us—that we are not alone—bring peace. As we accept the "rests" in our lives, we find that the blessings we were too busy to receive before bring a new joy.

In an old bookstore I recently found the journal of a lady who had lived in the early nineteenth century. The writing was faded, but as I began to decipher it, I saw that she had been a person of great faith. There were many quotations about God and His goodness to her. Over the years, her writing changed from that of a young woman to one who had grown elderly: I saw that more and more she depended on the Lord. On almost the last page she wrote:

> *Peace, that speaks the heavenly Giver,*
> *Peace, to worldly minds unknown.*
> *Peace—choice—that lasts forever,*
> *Peace, that comes from God alone.*

This nineteenth–century lady, who must have faced the same fears about illness that we face today, knew the secret of serenity: a simple trust in the One who had created her. She found that all that mattered was knowing His presence was with her.

"Peace I leave with you, my peace I give unto you: not as the world giveth, give I unto you. Let not your heart be troubled, neither let it be afraid." (Jn. 14:27)

One Day We'll Be Reunited

—

FRIENDSHIPS can have a way of enriching us. One such friendship that I cherished was with Corrie ten Boom, the dedicated, loving Dutch lady, who, during World War II, had been imprisoned by the Nazis because of her courageous work in hiding and saving so many Jews. The horrors of Ravensbruck concentration camp had been real to her. In prison, she had lost many members of her family.

I was always enriched spiritually in her presence. Her eyes danced like the sparkling blue water of the Mediterranean Sea, and over and over again I heard her say, "The best is yet to be!" *Tante* Corrie saw beyond all the heartache to the time when she would be reunited with her family in heaven.

One day, after she had finished speaking to a large crowd, we began to walk out of the auditorium when a woman approached her and asked quite abruptly, "Why did God allow you to suffer in a concentration camp, and why did He allow your family to die?"

I waited for a profound answer to these questions: but *Tante* Corrie's reply was simple in its childlike faith.

"I don't know," she said, quietly. "But one day I will know—when I go to heaven, to be with my Lord. I shall ask Him. I know I shall be reunited with my family." Then again that positive statement—"The best is yet to be!"

The woman was taken aback for a moment. Then, seeing the sincerity in *Tante* Corrie's eyes, she accepted her answer.

A few months before Corrie ten Boom died, I went to the hospital to visit her. *Tante* Corrie had suffered greatly, but her eyes still shone radiantly. Her speech was now gone, and when I sat by her bed—not knowing quite what to say—I took her hand and simply whispered, "Jesus." Her face lit up and she managed to raise her other hand and point heavenward. Her faith was as strong as ever.

I asked her, *"Tante* Corrie, will you introduce me to Papa and Betsie and all your family when we get to Heaven?"

Tante Corrie nodded and smiled again. She looked at me with the confidence of one who unwaveringly believed she would be reunited with her family once more. God had prepared a place for the ten Boom family—there was no doubt.

"...so shall we ever be with the Lord." (I Thes. 4:17)

The same confidence that Corrie ten Boom had can be ours. For those of us who live in the Lord there is only a temporary parting.

An old German motto states, "Those who live in the Lord never see each other for the last time."

Bereavement comes to all of us. And no matter how firmly we believe in God's promise of eternal life through His Son, there is the heartwrenching experience of having a loved one leave us. Where there has been the warmth of their presence, there is emptiness.

Loved ones and friends can help us over the lonely days with their quiet understanding and love. But there always comes a time when we have to face the parting by ourselves. We have to go on living.

In the loneliest hours God comes to us, as He has promised.

"...lo, I am with you alway, even unto the end of the world..." (Matt. 28:20)

I remember when my father died someone said to me, "He's with God, Joan, and God is nearer to us than even our own breathing."

These words consoled me and still do, for God has been my Comforter and I have His promise that I'll see my earthly father again—and all those whom I have loved who have gone before me, in the Lord. Like Corrie ten Boom, I know that one day we'll be reunited.

Circling our world is the everlasting hope that Jesus Christ is alive! His victory over death, and His promise that one day He will be returning to this earth involves each one of us. Parting is not the end, but a triumphant beginning—forever with Him.

"And God shall wipe away all tears from their eyes; and there shall be no more death, neither sorrow, nor crying, neither shall there be any more pain: for the former things are passed away." (Rev. 21:4)

Book design by Elizabeth Woll
Type set in Meridien